Yellowstone's Cycle of Fire

Yellowstone's Cycle of Fire

A Carolrhoda Earth Watch Book

by Frank Staub

Carolrhoda Books, Inc./Minneapolis

For my parents, who knew fire during the summer of 1988.

Text copyright ©1993 by Frank Staub.

Photo Credits
Photographs courtesy of: cover, pp. 2, 21-24, Jim Peaco, Yellowstone National Park; pp. 8, 19, 25, 27, Jeff Henry, Yellowstone National Park; p. 18, Yellowstone National Park. All other photographs by Frank Staub.

LIBRARY OF CONGRESS CATALOGING-IN-PUBLICATION DATA

Staub, Frank.
  Yellowstone's Cycle of Fire / by Frank Staub
    p. cm.
  "A Carolrhoda earth watch book."
  Includes index.
  Summary: Describes the dramatic forest fires in Yellowstone National Park during the summer of 1988 and the subsequent renewal of the land.
  ISBN 0-87614-778-3
  1. Forest fires—Yellowstone National Park—Juvenile literature.
2. Fire ecology—Yellowstone National Park—Juvenile literature.
3. Yellowstone National Park—Juvenile literature. [1. Forest fires—Yellowstone National Park. 2. Fire ecology. 3. Ecology.
4. Yellowstone National Park. 5. National parks and reserves.]
I. Title.
  SD421.32.Y45S73 1993
  574.5'2642'0978752—dc20
                                          92-29631
                                              CIP
                                               AC

Manufactured in the United States of America

1 2 3 4 5 6 – P/JR – 98 97 96 95 94 93

METRIC CONVERSION CHART		
To find measurements that are almost equal		
WHEN YOU KNOW:	MULTIPLY BY:	TO FIND:
feet	30.48	centimeters
yards	0.91	meters
miles	1.61	kilometers

Contents:

Smoke over the Gardiner River, northern Yellowstone National Park, summer, 1988

Burned forest and Old Faithful

A Summer of Smoke and Flames

When most Americans hear the words "national park" they think of Yellowstone. Located in the Rocky Mountains of Wyoming, Idaho, and Montana, Yellowstone National Park is the world's oldest national park and the biggest park in the United States outside of Alaska. It's also one of the most popular parks. Each year over two million people visit Yellowstone to see the earth's largest concentration of geysers shoot hot water and steam from underground high into the air. People also come because Yellowstone is one of the best places in the country to see large wild animals in their natural habitats. It's no wonder we call Yellowstone "The Crown Jewel" of our national park system.

7

When much of Yellowstone was burned by forest fires during the summer of 1988, America regarded it as a national tragedy. The story made national news throughout the summer. At times, lines of flames a mile wide raced across the land as fast as a person could walk. Veteran fire fighters had never seen anything so furious. All they could do was evacuate people, hose down buildings, and pray for rain. But rain didn't come. On August 20, or "Black Saturday," as it was called, more acres burned in one day than during any decade since the park was established in 1872.

Fire nears the parking lot at Old Faithful, summer, 1988.

Tourists watch Old Faithful and the smoke from a nearby forest fire (top right of photograph).

In the end, the Yellowstone fires struck one-third of the park and resulted in the most costly fire-fighting effort the United States had ever seen. But as the smoke cleared and the tourists returned, they found that the animals and geysers were still there. The tourists also found millions of blackened tree trunks and dense patches of wildflowers. This strange landscape, previously seen only by Native Americans from Yellowstone's past, marked the beginning of a new era in Yellowstone.

9

How It Happened

To understand the events leading up to the fires of 1988, we have to look at the history of fire in Yellowstone. Scientists learned of Yellowstone's fire history by looking at fire scars left on the trees. A fire scar forms when one side of a tree burns deep enough to kill the living cells under the bark. If enough cells are left alive on the tree's unburned side, the tree will survive. But it is scarred for life.

Fire Signs from the Past

By removing a wood sample from a fire-scarred tree and counting the growth rings, scientists can tell when a fire took place. Each ring represents one year of growth. Growth rings will not form over a fire scar. But the number of rings in the unscarred part of the tree still indicate the tree's age.

To determine the year a fire occurred the scientists use simple arithmetic. First, they subtract the age of the tree when the scar formed from the tree's current age. Then they subtract that number from the current year. The result is the year the fire occurred.

A scientist examines a fire scar on a tree in Yellowstone.

Ancient trees in Yellowstone that have turned to stone, or become petrified, contain the scars of prehistoric fires.

After determining the dates of many ancient fires from the scars they left on the trees, scientists found that over the centuries small fires have been common in Yellowstone. They also discovered that large fires burned thousands of acres around 1700 and again in the mid-1800s. From this, scientists were able to predict that Yellowstone was due for a large fire.

The trees themselves are one reason large fires are rare in Yellowstone's forests. The region's most common tree, the lodgepole pine, doesn't catch fire easily because it doesn't have branches low to the ground.

In Yellowstone, a lodgepole **stand** may live 250 to 400 years. During the first century of the stand's existence, surface fires are unable to climb into the treetops, or forest **canopy**, where they could explode into tree-killing blazes. That's because lodgepoles are **self-pruning**—the lower branches die and drop off as the tree grows taller. This makes the lodgepole resemble a skinny telephone pole topped with a Christmas tree. Since there are no lower branches to catch fire, a surface fire cannot "ladder up" a lodgepole's trunk to the forest canopy.

Two other common trees on the Yellowstone Plateau are the Engelmann spruce and the subalpine fir. Unlike pines, which need plenty of sunlight, spruces and firs tolerate shade. They can sprout on the dark floor of a lodgepole forest where few other plants grow.

Slowly, the spruces and firs grow tall and replace the lodgepoles as they die. This process of one plant species taking over another plant species is called **plant succession**. Young lodgepoles will not develop in the shade of the spruces and firs because the lodgepoles require direct sunlight. So most of Yellowstone's lodgepole forests will eventually turn into forests of spruces and firs—if there aren't any fires for two or three hundred years.

A lodgepole forest, well over 100 years old, with a spruce and fir understory

Before the change from lodgepole forest to spruce-fir forest is complete, lightning usually ignites a fire. The spruce and fir trees then become ladders to their own destruction because, unlike lodgepole pines, spruces and firs are not self-pruning. They keep their lower branches. This allows flames to spread from branch to branch up the trunks, as if they were climbing a ladder, and **crown-out** into the forest canopy. If the weather is dry, and if there is enough wind, the fire will quickly spread through the canopy of the entire stand.

The floor of this mature lodgepole forest is littered with dry, dead trees and branches.

A herd of bison weather the winter in Yellowstone.

The cold, wet weather at Yellowstone is another reason there is a long time between fires. Most of Yellowstone consists of mountains and the Yellowstone Plateau. The plateau makes up most of the park. Its average elevation is about 8,000 feet above sea level. At this altitude, there's plenty of rain and snow to keep the twigs, branches, and pine needles on the forest floor moist throughout the summer. So even if a fire does get started, it rarely burns very far. But, from 1982 to 1988, winter snowfall was below average. Yellowstone's forests slowly dried out.

The summer of 1988 began like other summers. April and May were rainy. Lightning ignited the usual number of forest fires. Many went out on their own. But almost no rain fell in July and August. It was one of the driest summers in the park's 116-year history. In addition, temperatures were unusually high. The heat and lack of moisture caused the fallen trees and branches on the forest floor to become as dry as the boards in a lumberyard. The combination of a hot, dry summer and old forests with dry understories made a large fire inevitable.

A surface fire races through a mature lodgepole forest beside the Madison River, August, 1988.

Fighting the Fires

When the first fires of 1988 began in Yellowstone, the Park Service responded with its "Natural Burn" policy. This policy states that fires started accidentally by humans must be suppressed immediately. Discarded cigarette butts, fallen power lines, and unattended campfires are common causes of forest fires.

But the Natural Burn policy also states that fires caused by lightning from thunderstorms have been an important part of Yellowstone's natural ecology for thousands of years. By law, natural events such as lightning-caused fires are protected in a national park. These kinds of fires are allowed to burn—unless they threaten human life and property.

Some people call the Natural Burn policy the "Let It Burn" policy, but this is misleading. Park officials don't just let a lightning-caused fire burn. They watch it closely. If the fire looks as if it might become dangerous, they classify it as a "wildfire" and put it out, or at least try to keep it from spreading.

By mid-July 1988, all fires in Yellowstone were regarded as wildfires. They were spreading so rapidly that park officials decided to suppress every fire no matter what its cause. (Human-caused fires in and around the park were already being fought.) Based on past experience, the officials thought the burning would be brought quickly under control. They were wrong.

During the height of the Yellowstone fires, over 9,000 men and women from as far away as Hawaii and Florida were employed to battle the blazes. They used 100 fire trucks, dozens of aircraft, 10 million gallons of water, and 1½ million gallons of **fire retardants**.

Fighting forest fires is a tough, dirty job. But the work can be very satisfying, and it pays well. A fire fighter's day may last 12 to 14 hours. He or she must often hike 10 miles or more carrying a canteen, headlamp, first aid kit, gloves, goggles, and heavy tools. Fireproof clothing protects fire fighters from the flames but not from the intense heat. Nor does it protect them from bee stings, sunburn, and grizzly bears.

One of the most important pieces of equipment a fire fighter carries is an emergency fire shelter. The shelter looks like a tent made of thick aluminum foil. Fortunately, these "brown and serve" bags, as fire fighters call them, are rarely needed because a fire crew always tries to identify a **safe spot** where they can go if the flames get too close. A safe spot may be a clearing, a rocky area, parking lot, or some other place that won't burn. During the summer of 1988, a crew of 18 was caught in the middle of a grass fire to the northeast of Yellowstone for 15 minutes with no safe spot. Although some of the men were burned, their emergency shelters saved their lives.

The computer is another fire-fighting tool. Computers were used to predict where the Yellowstone fires would go and how long they would take to get there. But the fires spread much faster than the predictions said they would. By early August, there were over a dozen major fires burning throughout the park.

Fire fighters digging fire lines

One of the fire fighters' main tasks was constructing **fire lines**. A fire line is a strip of ground from which all the plants and burnable ground cover have been scraped away. When the advancing flames reach a fire line, they have nothing to burn and usually go out. But the relentless winds in Yellowstone during the summer of 1988 caused the flames to blow across fire lines. This made the men and women fighting the fires feel like soldiers losing a war. Near the end of the summer, real soldiers and marines were brought in to relieve the weary fire fighters.

The summer of 1988 was Yellowstone's windiest summer on record. Gusts of 40 miles per hour were common. These winds not only fanned the flames but also promoted **spotting**—new flare-ups caused by hot embers blown up to 1½ miles away from the main blazes. Continual spotting made it easy for the fires to cross rivers, canyons, geyser fields, and other areas that usually stop advancing flames. Furthermore, unlike most forest fires, which die down after dark, the Yellowstone fires of 1988 maintained their fury around the clock.

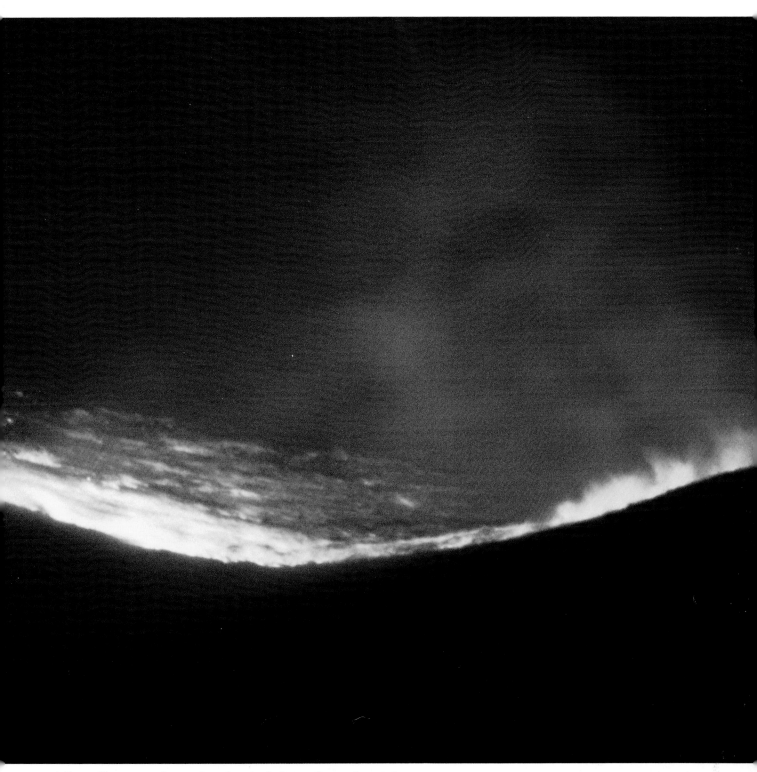

The Yellowstone fires often burned throughout the night.

A fire storm

Numerous **fire storms** made fighting the fires especially difficult. A fire storm is a swirling, roaring tower of flame. Scientists estimate that a fire storm releases as much energy every 15 minutes as a small atomic bomb. A fire storm develops when hot air rises rapidly from a large fire. This causes air to be sucked in from below at speeds great enough to topple trees. The only thing humans can do when faced with such an inferno is remove logs, branches, pine needles, and other fuels from the fire's path and hope it will burn itself out.

As the fires spread, many people argued that Yellowstone's Natural Burn policy was responsible. But this policy played only a minor role. Most of the burning resulted from fires caused by humans—not lightning. These were fought as soon as they were detected. In fact, the North Fork Fire, which was responsible for over half the burn area inside the park, was started outside the park when careless woodcutters dropped burning cigarette butts.

Most experts now agree that even if the Yellowstone fires had not been fought at all, the amount of land burned would have been about the same. Donald Hodel, who was secretary of the interior under President Ronald Reagan at the time, described the situation in the following way: "It's like the guy who takes an 800-pound gorilla for a walk and is asked the question, 'Where do you walk him?' The answer: 'Anywhere he wants to go.' That's how the fire was. Once it got started, it went anywhere it wanted to go."

A plane drops fire retardant

The Aftermath

It wasn't until snow fell in September that the Yellowstone fires were finally brought under control. Some burning continued until November 13. By then, approximately one-third of the park's 2.2 million acres had been affected—a total of 793,000 acres inside the park and another 600,000 in the national forests and other lands nearby.

These numbers are misleading because not all the land in a "burn area" actually burns. Rather, a burn area is generally a mixture of totally burned, partially burned, and unburned sections that together are called a **burn mosaic**.

The most noticeable parts of a burn mosaic are the canopy burns formed when flames reach all the way to the highest branches. In a canopy burn, all the trees and ground cover are killed. About half of the burn areas in Yellowstone during 1988 were canopy burns.

An area of almost equal size were surface burns. Surface burns consume mainly the fallen branches and needles on the forest floor. The trees may be scorched in a surface burn, but they are rarely killed.

Burn mosaic on Bunsen Peak

Hosing down the Old Faithful Inn

The Yellowstone fires were fascinating to watch from a distance. But they did cause hardships for many people. A total of 65 buildings and other structures, and about 200 power-line poles were destroyed. The estimated cost of the damage was $3,280,000. Two people died in the fires, both were fire fighters. One was struck by a falling **snag**—a tree that had been killed by fire. The other died in a helicopter accident.

It was surprising that more people weren't killed, considering the thousands of people living in five towns along the park's borders, as well as those in the campgrounds, hotels, and cabins inside the park, who had to be evacuated at least once. As the flames closed in, heavy dousings with water and flame-retardant foam saved many buildings, such as the historic Old Faithful Inn.

Many people worried that the fires would harm the park's wild animals. Some of Yellowstone's small animals, such as snakes and crawling insects, did perish in the fires. But others, like the pocket gopher and the badger, hid safely underground in their burrows until the flames passed over them. Birds simply flew to safe perches.

Most of the large animals, for which the park is so famous, were able to walk away when the fires got too close. Bison and elk were often seen grazing in meadows next to burning forests.

A total of 257 of Yellowstone Park's elk and 9 of its bison died because of the fires. These numbers are small compared to the total herd sizes of approximately 30,000 elk and 2,000 bison.

In addition, four deer, two black bears, and two moose died because of fires in the park during the summer of 1988. Fire retardant was accidentally dropped in streams and killed some fish. Noise from fire-fighting aircraft probably disturbed many animals but no endangered species died in the fires.

A pocket gopher burrow in a burned forest

Bison scratching on a burned log

Bison herd and smoke on the North Range during the 1988 fires

Smoke inhalation was the leading cause of animal death. Smoke from Yellowstone was visible as far away as Minnesota, and even from outer space. The smoke posed health problems for nearby communities as well. Visitors with breathing problems were warned to stay away. Drivers had to keep their headlights on during the day. At times, breathing the smokey air was like smoking four packs of cigarettes a day. The great clouds of smoke also made it hard for fire-fighting pilots to see.

This elk died the first winter after the fires.

The first winter after the fires was difficult for Yellowstone's animals. Large numbers of elk and bison died because so much of their winter food supply had been burned or killed by drought. Park officials decided not to feed the starving animals because artificial feeding discourages them from seeking wild food sources on their own. It also causes the animals to concentrate their populations where the feeding occurs. Close concentration of animal populations sometimes leads to the rapid spread of disease. And after the feeding program is stopped, the local vegetation becomes damaged because so many animals have grazed in one small area.

The animal deaths during the winter of 1989 may seem like a tragedy, but winter-killed animals help to maintain the **balance of nature** in Yellowstone. At the beginning of 1989 there were too many elk and bison for the available food supply. When there isn't enough food for all the animals in an environment, the balance of nature is changed. All living things are affected by other living things. They must maintain a balance with each other for their communities to survive. The six winters leading up to the 1988 fires had been milder than usual. This allowed older animals, which would have otherwise perished, to live. But the winter of 1989 was more typically harsh. With much of the usual food supply gone, the balance of nature shifted, and the very old animals became too weak to survive.

Eagles, ravens, magpies, coyotes, grizzly bears, and other scavengers benefitted by feeding on the carcasses of winter-killed animals. The abundance of food in the form of dead elk may explain the large number of grizzly bear cubs born during the first year after the fires.

Yellowstone's grizzly bears grew fat by feeding on the carcasses of winter-killed animals.

Up From the Ashes

Most of Yellowstone's animals survived the winter following the fires. Then, during the spring and summer, the animals quickly fattened up as the burn areas became carpeted with the grasses and wildflowers they love to eat. Some grasses appeared on the burn sites just weeks after the flames passed through.

About two dozen different kinds of plants, as well as tiny tree seedlings, soon began to grow out of the ashes. Many of these plants already existed before the fires. But they were not visible because they had very few stems and leaves—just roots.

Roots absorb water and **nutrients** from the soil for use by the entire plant. Nutrients are minerals such as nitrogen, phosphorus, potassium, magnesium, and calcium. They are necessary for plant growth. Leaves take energy from sunlight and use it to make much of the food that nourishes most plants. Stems hold up the leaves and send water, nutrients, and other chemicals between the leaves and the roots.

The roots of certain plants have a second job. They store food during times when the plants' leaves are missing. The roots of some plants can even sprout (send up new stems and leaves) on their own. These roots allow forest plants to survive long periods when little sunlight filters through the treetops.

One plant that sends up stems and leaves from its roots is fireweed, so named because it is very common after a fire. Roots of a fireweed plant can live beneath a forest floor for many years. When fire comes, the soil protects the roots and allows them to survive. After the fire, the fireweed's true abundance is revealed as hundreds of small plants spring forth. All that is needed is enough sunlight for the fireweed to make the food required to develop into complete plants.

Fireweed is one of the first plants to appear after a fire.

An elk feeds on fireweed in a burned forest.

Many of the plants that appeared on the burn sites sprouted from seeds rather than roots. Some of the seeds blew in from unburned areas. Others were carried to the burn sites on the fur of animals or in animal droppings. Still other seeds were in the soil before the fires occurred, waiting years, in some cases, for the flood of sunshine that follows fire.

Warmth is another reason for the post-fire surge in plant growth. The charred earth takes on a darker color and absorbs more light energy, which then changes into heat energy. The soil and the roots warm up. The warmth then increases the rate at which the roots absorb nutrients.

Nutrients absorbed by trees may stay in the trees' bodies for many years, even after the trees die. A process called **nutrient recycling** returns them to the earth. Bacteria, fungi, and other **decomposer organisms** are the nutrient recyclers in most natural environments. They eat the dead plants and put the nitrates, phosphates, potassium, magnesium, and calcium from the plants' bodies back into the soil. In this way, the nutrients are used over and over again as part of a natural cycle.

Decomposer organisms work best in warm weather. But the high Yellowstone Plateau, where nighttime temperatures may fall below freezing even in summer, is often too cold for decomposers to have much of an effect. So the plants depend on fire for nutrient recycling.

As the forest burns, minerals locked in the trees and other plants are suddenly released back into the soil. After the fires of 1988, large sections of Yellowstone's nutrient-poor earth received a tremendous flood of nutrients that will nourish its forests for many years to come.

Asters thrive in the nutrient-rich soil after a fire.

Nutrient recycling is one of the ways fire maintains nature's balance. But this balance is very delicate. Although plants need the nutrients recycled by fire, too many nutrients can be harmful. Wherever logs and piles of dead pine needles burned for long periods of time, so many minerals were released that the soil became temporarily poisoned. Seeds could not sprout in these places until rain and melting snow watered down the nutrients to the proper levels.

Deep heating also caused slower regrowth on these areas. The smoldering logs and plant materials steadily released heat, which penetrated one inch or more into the soil—deep enough to kill roots, seeds, and other underground plant parts. During the first summer after the fires, these areas of deep heating and excess nutrients were highly visible as light-colored spots and strips amid the dark soil. However, they accounted for less than one percent of the total burn area.

Left: A four-year-old lodgepole grows next to a burned lodgepole.
Inset: Serotinous lodgepole pine cones

When fire destroys a forest on the Yellowstone Plateau or in the nearby mountains, lodgepole pines are usually the first trees to reappear. That's because the bare, sunlit soil that remains after a fire is exactly the kind of environment in which lodgepole seedlings grow best.

Lodgepoles also come back quickly after a fire because of their special **serotinous cones**. A serotinous cone is coated with a hard waxy substance. The temperature must reach at least 113°F for this substance to become soft enough for the cone to open and release its seeds. Due to Yellowstone's cool temperatures, fire is the only source of this kind of heat.

Lodgepoles also produce ordinary cones that open and shed their seeds on a regular basis without heat. But the fire-sensitive serotinous cones may remain unopened for many years. The tree branches hold more and more of them as time passes. Then, after a fire, many new trees are produced even if the original tree is killed.

Some of the areas burned in 1988 contained a million seeds per acre. Of these seeds, about 750 sprouted to form tree seedlings on each acre of land. With such an abundance of new lodgepoles, the park service saw little need to plant trees in the burn areas. For the most part, Yellowstone's forests replanted themselves, just as they have after fires in the past.

Dense regrowth on the forest floor.
Inset: The glacier lily is common
after fire.

At first, the tiny lodgepoles were hard to see amid the fireweed, asters, lupine, elk sedge, and two dozen other plant species that grew on the burn sites. Many young lodgepoles died because they didn't get enough sunlight, water, or nutrients. But within 10 years after a canopy burn, what was once a flowery meadow starts to look like a forest, as waist-high trees become the dominant plants. After about 50 years, the new trees grow to heights of 20-30 feet.

A hundred years or so after a fire, the trees are 30 to 50 feet high and form dense stands. As the trees grow taller, the forest canopy becomes thicker and eventually closes, blocking sunlight to the forest floor. With so little light, most of the colorful shrubs and wildflowers die off.

Other than Engelmann spruce and subalpine fir, very few plants can survive on the dark floor of a mature lodgepole forest. Scientists say that such a forest has low **biodiversity**—there is very little variety of plants and animals. In contrast, the first 20 years after a fire is a period of high biodiversity. In fact, the diversity of plant life during that period may be 10 times greater than it was before the forest burned.

If the biodiversity of an environment becomes too low, nature's balance is upset. If spaces weren't opened in the forest by periodic canopy burns, many of the plants that have lived in the Yellowstone area for thousands of years would die off completely. Without fire, most of Yellowstone would gradually change into a dark forest of only spruce and fir trees.

Fire also maintains Yellowstone's diversity of animal life. While the fires burned, large numbers of hawks and other birds of prey moved in to snatch up mice, voles, and other rodents suddenly left without cover. After the flames passed, seed-eating birds, such as pine siskins, Clark's nutcrackers, and red crossbills, feasted on the flood of lodgepole seeds released by the serotinous cones.

Later, beetles and other insects laid eggs in the burned tree snags. When the eggs hatched, woodpeckers, mountain bluebirds, robins, and other birds flew in from all over to feast on the young insects.

The snags also made good nesting sites. Mountain bluebirds and tree swallows mate mainly in the young forests that occur after fires. And the post-fire fields of grasses and wildflowers are ideal places for birds to feed on flying insects and for large animals to graze.

The Cycle of Fire

Due to the property damage caused by the 1988 fires, some changes have been made to Yellowstone's Natural Burn policy. Small, controlled surface fires are now started periodically near buildings to burn off dead trees and branches that might fuel a large-scale fire. Also, lightning-caused fires are watched even more closely than they were in the past. In very dry or windy years they will be suppressed more quickly.

In spite of the problems they caused, the Yellowstone fires did present many opportunities for us to gain new knowledge. Before 1988, almost all of our information about nature's response to fire came from relatively small burns. Now we are learning about the changes that occur when fire affects large areas of land.

The fires created a special opportunity for park visitors. At no other time during Yellowstone's long history as a national park has there been such a diversity of life. Nearly a third of its surface is now like a vast natural garden, where thousands of animals live without fear of humans.

Thanks to the fires of 1988, Yellowstone has entered a period of birth and regrowth that will continue through the twenty-first century. And although this period may not be as exciting as the fires themselves, it is just as fascinating. As Park Supervisor Bob Barbee put it, "Nature is not always a gentle hostess, but she never fails to be an inspiring teacher." As a teacher, nature in the form of fire has been an important part of our world for a very long time.

GLOSSARY

balance of nature: all living things have effects on each other that must be in balance for each to survive

biodiversity: a variety of different kinds of plants and animals

burn mosaic: an area of burned land that is made up of totally burned, partially burned, and unburned sections

canopy: the top of a tree

crown-out: when fire reaches the canopy

decomposer organisms: organisms, such as bacteria and fungi, that eat dead plants, breaking down the plants' nutrients and returning them to the soil

fire lines: a strip of ground where all burnable materials have been removed

fire retardants: materials used to slow or stop fires

fire storm: a swirling, roaring fire of great intensity caused by hot air rising rapidly from a large fire

nutrient recycling: the process of nutrients from dead plants returning to the soil where they become food for new plants

nutrients: minerals that are necessary for plant and animal growth

plant succession: the process of one kind of plant taking over the living area of another kind of plant

safe spot: a place where fire won't burn

self-pruning: the lower branches of the tree drop off as the tree grows taller

serotinous cones: a cone coated with a hard waxy substance that must melt for the cone to open and release its seeds

snag: a tree that has been killed by fire

spotting: new fires caused by hot embers carried away from a fire by wind

stand: a group of trees growing next to each other

INDEX

ABOUT THE AUTHOR

Frank Staub is the author of several books for children and dozens of magazine articles. He holds degrees in Biology and Zoology. He works as a freelance writer and photographer, which allows him to travel to and study the places and events that intrigue him most. When he's not working, he competes in running and bicycle races, climbs mountains, and enjoys sea kayaking.